AMAZING ACTIVITIES FOR

MINECRAFTERS

Puzzles and Games for Hours of Entertainment!

Sky Pony Press
New York

Sky Pony Press books may be purchased in bulk at special discounts for sales promotion, corporate gifts, fund-raising, or educational purposes. Special editions can also be created to specifications. For details, contact the Special Sales Department, Sky Pony Press, 307 West 36th Street, 11th Floor, New York, NY 10018 or info@skyhorsepublishing.com.

Sky Pony® is a registered trademark of Skyhorse Publishing, Inc.®, a Delaware corporation.

Minecraft® is a registered trademark of Notch Development AB.
The Minecraft game is copyright © Mojang AB.

Visit our website at www.skyponypress.com.

15 14 13 12 11 10 9 8

Library of Congress Cataloging-in-Publication Data is available on file.

Puzzles created by Jen Funk Weber
Cover and interior design by Kevin Baier
Cover and interior illustrations by Amanda Brack

Print ISBN: 978-1-5107-2174-6

Printed in China

TABLE OF CONTENTS

GOING BATTY

There are fourteen bats hidden in this Minecrafter's haunted house.
Can you find them all without going batty?

STEVE SAYS...

If you have ever played the game Simon Says, then you know how this game works: follow only the directions that begin with "Steve says" to reveal a fun fact for Minecrafters.

	1	2	3	4	5
A	SPIDERS	ONE	CREEPERS	CREATE	MAGENTA
B	WERE	SILVERFISH	MAKE	VILLAGERS	THE
C	OCELOT	RESULT	CONSTRUCT	GREEN	OF
D	PINK	IS	A	FOREST	SAVANNA
E	CODING	PURPLE	THE	MISTAKE	BE

1. **Steve says,** "Cross off all the Mobs in Row B and Column 1."

2. **Steve says,** "Cross off all colors."

3. **Steve says,** "Cross off all biomes."

4. Cross off nouns (people, places, things) in Column 4.

5. **Steve says,** "Cross off synonyms of 'build' in Columns 3 and 4."

6. **Steve says,** "Cross off words with four or fewer letters in Column 2 and Row E."

7. **Steve says,** "Read the remaining words to reveal a fact about the game."

THE MIRROR'S IMAGE

Circle letters on the top half of the grid that have correct mirror images on the bottom half. Write the circled letters in order on the spaces provided to reveal a cool fact about Endermen.

```
E  I  M  N  D  N  E  O  R  T  M  E  K  N  W  I  E  R  E  D
C  A  L  D  L  I  E  D  F  N  A  G  R  Y  L  A  N  O  D  E
U  R  P  S  B  E  U  Z  F  O  R  Z  L  E  T  E  H  E  P  E
N  E  D  W  R  A  S  S  C  R  O  E  A  T  N  E  Y  D  O  U
```

```
Ͷ  ∩  D  W  S  A  S  C  Я  E  A  ʈ  O  E  D  I  E  T
Я  Я  E  S  B  E  A  ⅄  O  Я  B  ∩  E  ⅃  T  H  E  O  E
C  A  T  T  Λ  E  D  E  A  Я  Я  S  T  A  Ͷ  A  D  E
E  D  ∩  Ͷ  S  E  S  Я  T  W  E  E  Ͷ  S  E  Я  O
```

__ __ __ __ __ __ __ __ __ __ __ __ __ __ __ __ __

" __ __ __ __ __ __ __ __ __ __ " __ __ __ __ __ __ __ __

__ __ __ __ __ __ __ __ __ __ __ __ __

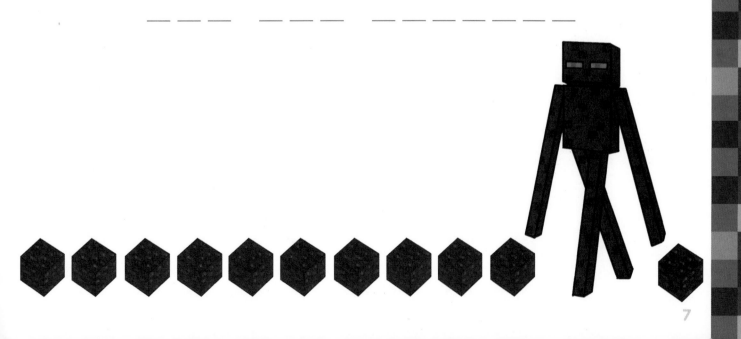

CITY SLICKER

A highly-skilled Minecrafter built the first city below. She logged back in later and made ten changes to her city. Look at the second city on the opposite page. Can you identify all ten changes?

TAKE A GUESS

Write the answers to the clues on the numbered spaces, one letter on each blank. Then transfer the letters to the boxes with the same numbers. A few have already been done for you! If you fill in the boxes correctly, you'll reveal something very useful for Minecrafters.

The way out

$\frac{}{10} \frac{x}{2} \frac{}{6} \frac{}{15}$

This grows on ears and is sometimes popped

$\frac{}{9} \frac{}{12} \frac{r}{5} \frac{}{8}$

A kind of tree

$\frac{p}{11} \frac{}{13} \frac{}{14} \frac{}{1}$

To leak through

$\frac{s}{16} \frac{}{4} \frac{}{7} \frac{}{3}$

1	2	3	4	5	6	7	8	9	10
	x			r					

11	12	13	14	15	16
p					s

ENCHANTED CHEST

This End City chest is enchanted. To open it, you must press all nine buttons just once, in the correct order.

Follow the directions on the buttons. For instance, 2D means you must move your finger two buttons down. R=right. L=left. U=up. To open the chest, you must land on the F button last.

Which button do you have to press first to land on the F button last?

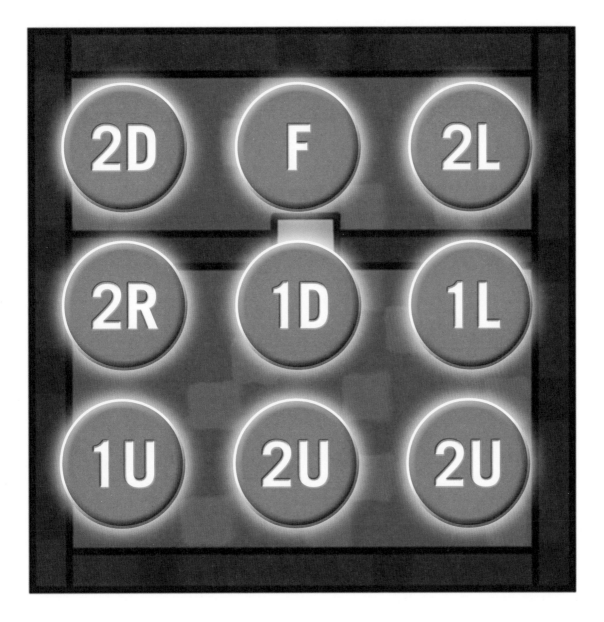

SEE AND SOLVE

In this crossword puzzle, you get to figure out where each word fits! Use the picture clues to guess the word answers, then see where each word fits best. If you fill in the puzzle correctly, you'll get a funny answer to the question below!

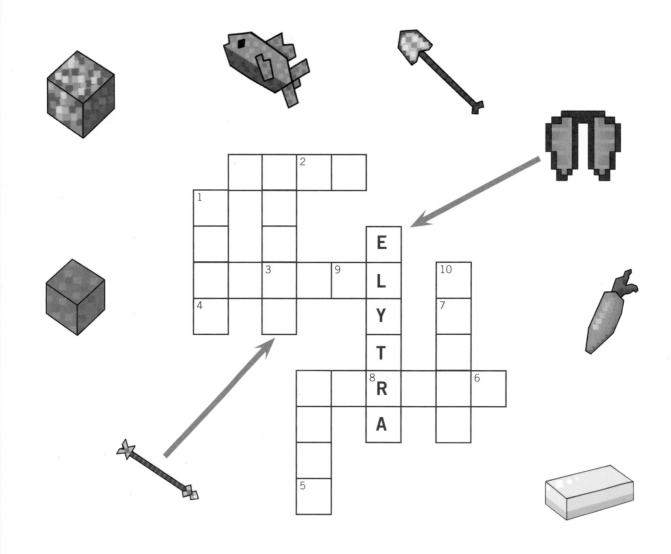

What happens when blazes are promoted to managers?

―― ―― ―― ――   ―― ―― ―― ――   ―― ―― ―― ―― ―― ―― ―― ――
 6 4 9 5   1 10 8 9   9 2 9 8 5 3 7 9

HOME SWEET BIOME

Find and circle the names of fourteen Minecraft biomes in the wordfind below. They might be forward, backward, up, down, or diagonal.

DEEP OCEAN
DESERT
EXTREME HILLS
FROZEN RIVER
JUNGLE

MUSHROOM ISLAND
NETHER
PLAINS
ROOFED FOREST
SAVANNA

STONE BEACH
SWAMPLAND
TAIGA
THE END

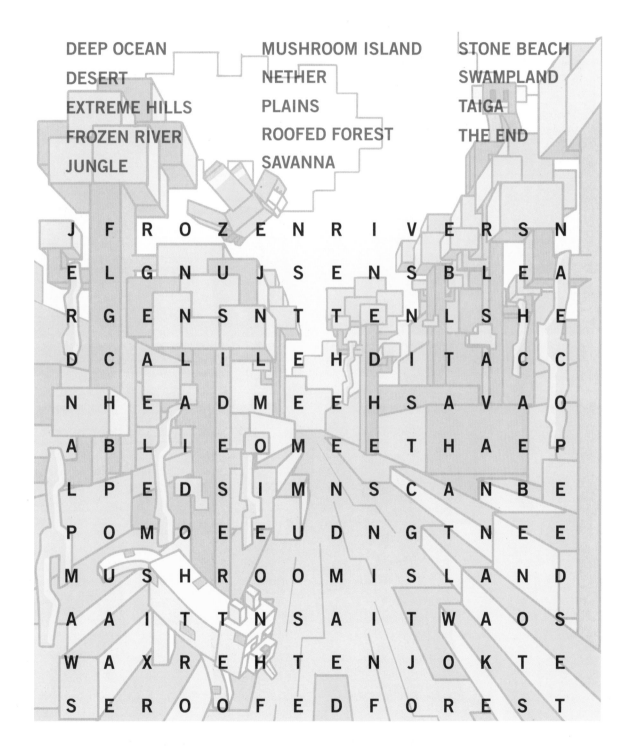

```
J F R O Z E N R I V E R S N
E L G N U J S E N S B L E A
R G E N S N T T E N L S H E
D C A L I L E H D I T A C C
N H E A D M E E H S A V A O
A B L I E O M E E T H A E P
L P E D S I M N S C A N B E
P O M O E E U D N G T N E E
M U S H R O O M I S L A N D
A A I T T N S A I T W A O S
W A X R E H T E N J O K T E
S E R O O F E D F O R E S T
```

CREEPER TWINS

Only two of these creepers are exactly the same. Which two are identical?

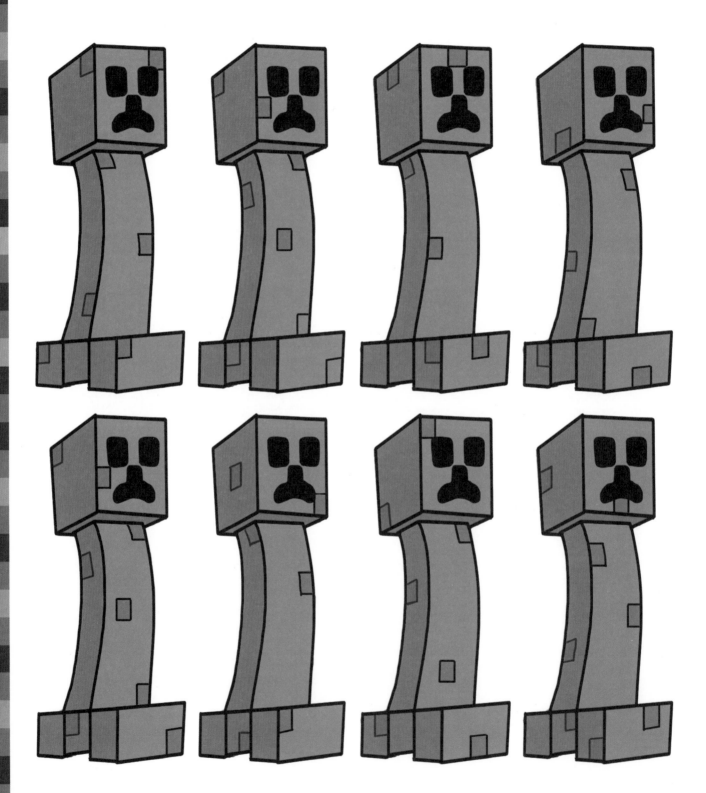

CIRCLE OF TRUTH: CRAFTING CLUE

Start at the ▼. Write every third letter on the spaces below to reveal a truth that all Minecrafters should know.

D _ _ _ _ _ _   _ _ _ _   _ _ _

_ _ _ _ _ _ _ _ _ _ _   _ _ _ _

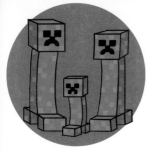

MOB SCENE

Write answers to the clues in the boxes. Read the highlighted boxes downward to reveal a phrase that describes a common Mob scene. Need a hint? The answers are scrambled around the border.

SONIE

RACESH

PALSEP

TOPUTU

1. To look for something
2. Someone with mad skills
3. Horses and pigs eat these
4. Another word for a Minecrafter
5. The opposite of *input*
6. Use this to ride a pig
7. The eye of this is poisonous and used in brewing
8. Another word for *sound*
9. Use this to spawn a chicken

DASLED

REVPAL

1.
2.
3.
4.
5.
6.
7.
8.
9.

GEG   REPEXT   DRISPE

SQUARED UP: MOBS IN EVERY QUARTER

Each of the four Mobs in this puzzle can appear only once in each row, each column, and the four inside boxes.

B = BABY ZOMBIE VILLAGERS

C = CREEPER

G = GHAST

S = SKELETON

G			B
B	S		
		B	S
	B		G

WATCHTOWER QUEST

Can you find your way back home to where you built the watchtower?

START

A CURE FOR WHAT AILS YOU

Boxes connected by lines contain the same letter. Some letters are given; others have to be guessed. Fill in all the boxes to reveal a piece of gaming advice.

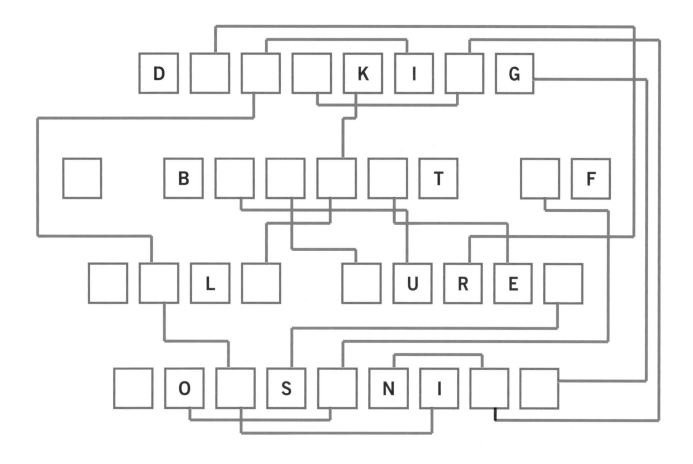

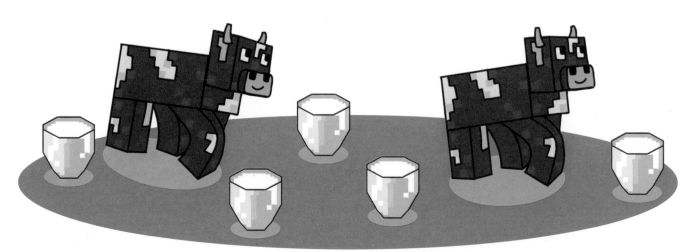

YOU CAN DRAW IT: WOLF

Use the grid to copy the picture one square at a time. Examine the lines in each small square in the top grid then transfer those lines to the corresponding square in the bottom grid. When you finish, you'll have drawn a wolf all your own!

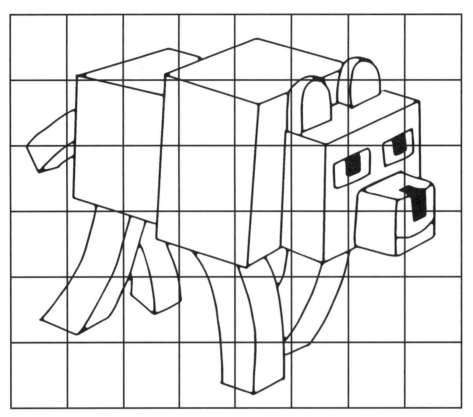

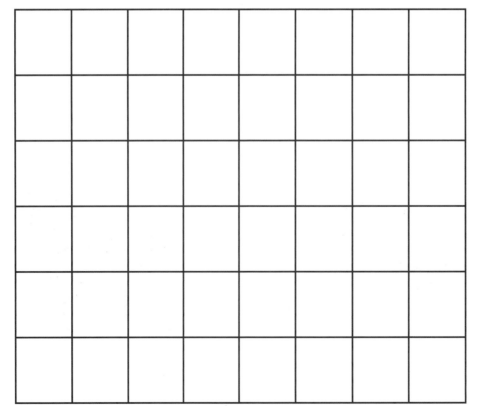

PIECE IT TOGETHER

Identify the seven green puzzle pieces that fit the shapes in the rectangle. Watch out! Pieces might be rotated or flipped. Write the letters of the correct pieces on each space. Not all the pieces will be used.

Read the letters you wrote to reveal the answer to the following question: **What Mobs make Steve and Alex tremble in fear?**

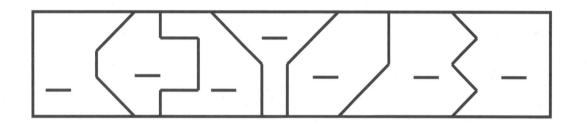

21

PICK, THE RIGHT TOOL!

There are thirteen pickaxes hidden in this toolshed. Can you pick them all out?

TOOL CHEST

Find and circle the names of nine Minecrafting tools in the letters. They might be forward, backward, up, down, or diagonal. Watch out! Every T, O, and L has been chipped away and replaced by a pickaxe. Can you find all nine tools?

CLOCK **FLINT AND STEEL** **PICKAXE**
COMPASS **IRON AXE** **SHEARS**
FISHING ROD **LEAD** **SHOVEL**

G K C ⛏ ⛏ C W E D ⛏ I S U

I M P E D ⛏ I R ⛏ N A X E

⛏ J B ⛏ S M S P A M ⛏ F H

V U P D N P F ⛏ X S G B ⛏

F ⛏ I N ⛏ A N D S ⛏ E E ⛏

P C C R E S Y U B Q V A N W

D W K ⛏ K S H A U ⛏ F C I

A ⛏ A U H V C E H K Y J R

E K X I ⛏ A N S A R ⛏ F ⛏

⛏ X E M U H ⛏ U C R M E I

A ⛏ S D ⛏ R G N I H S I F

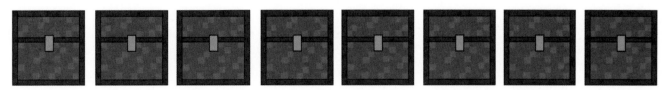

FIND THE PORTAL

Four players are racing to find the End portal. Only one will make it. Follow each player's path, under and over crossing paths, to discover who gets there and who hits a dead end.

Zombie94   Shtomp   Enchantress56   Gash

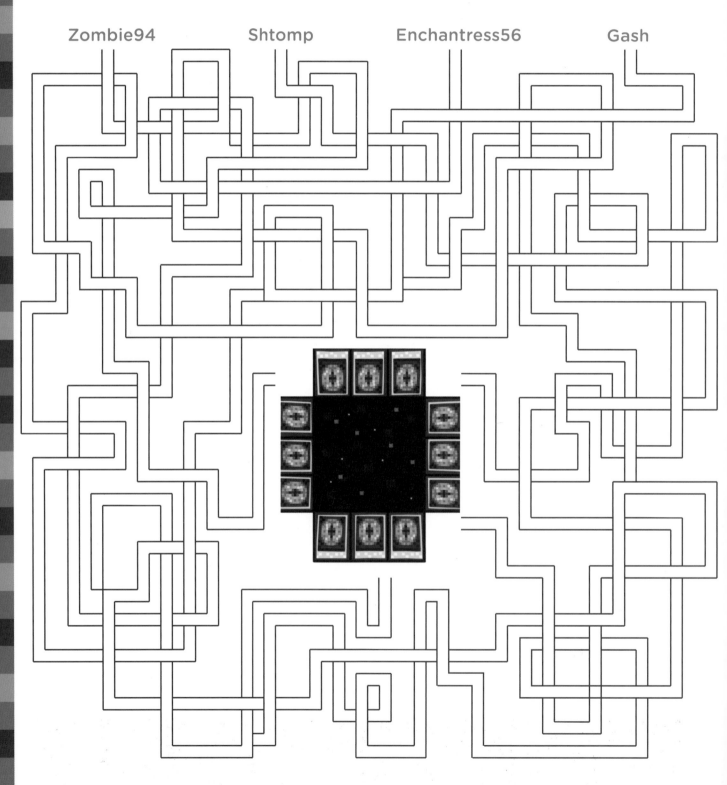

CROSSWORD CLUE FINDER

Use the pictures and arrows to help you fill in this crossword picture puzzle.
Some words can fit in more than one location, so choose carefully!

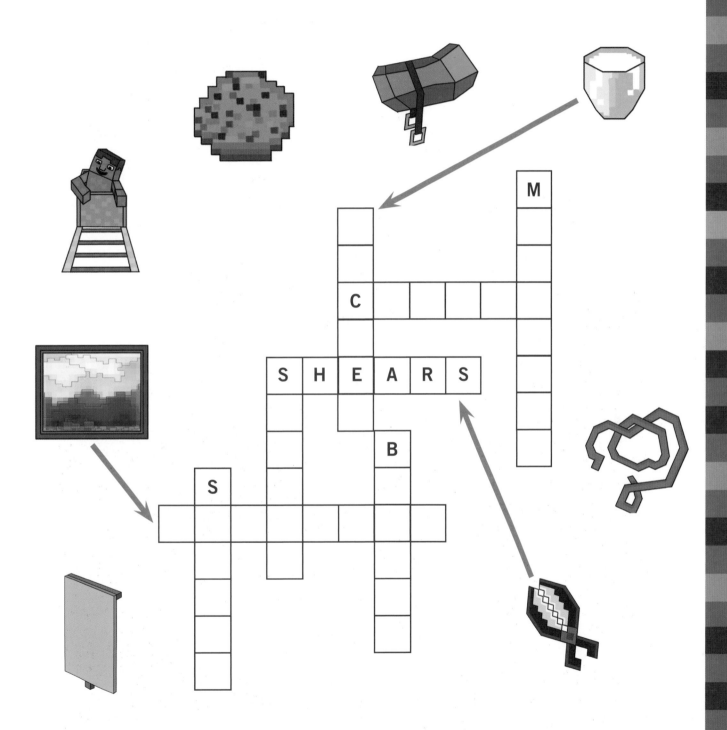

SEE THE SEA

These two pictures seem identical, but there are eleven differences between them. How many can you see?

POWER PLAY: MYSTERY WORD

Every word in Column B contains the same letters as a word in Column A, plus one letter. Draw a line between word "matches," then write the extra letter on the space provided. Unscramble the column of letters to reveal a powerful resource for Minecrafters.

COLUMN A	COLUMN B	EXTRA LETTER
Points	Steve	__
Healer	Diamond	__
Vest	Armor	__
Meander	Hardcore	__
Mentor	Potions	O
Domain	Monster	__
Roam	Enderman	__
Orchard	Leather	__

__ __ __ __ __ __ __ __ __

SURVIVAL MAZE

Find your way through this maze from Start to Finish
without bumping into a ghast, creeper, zombie, or skeleton.

Start

Finish

BLOCKED!

The names of fourteen Minecraft blocks are hidden below. They might be forward, backward, up, down, or diagonal. For an added challenge, some of the letters are blocked: every D, I, R, and T has been replaced by a ◼. Can you find all fourteen block names?

ANDESITE	GRANITE	OBSIDIAN
BEACON	LAPIS LAZULI	PRISMARINE
DIORITE	MONSTER EGG	PUMPKIN
EMERALD	MUSHROOM	SPONGE
GLOWSTONE	NETHER WART	

```
S  E  O  ◼  M  E  ◼  ◼  M  M  G  E
L  S  ◼  ◼  L  E  H  U  E  G  ◼  N
E  A  ◼  ◼  G  A  S  ◼  E  L  N  ◼
N  E  P  N  N  H  ◼  ◼  S  E  C  K
O  A  O  ◼  ◼  A  E  E  ◼  ◼  ◼  P
◼  P  ◼  O  S  ◼  ◼  H  M  E  ◼  M
S  E  O  ◼  S  L  E  G  N  E  O  U
W  M  E  N  ◼  ◼  A  M  S  ◼  ◼  P
O  ◼  O  ◼  W  S  S  Z  P  L  ◼  A
L  M  Y  A  S  M  B  ◼  U  N  ◼  C
G  E  ◼  B  E  A  C  O  N  L  E  ◼
E  ◼  ◼  S  E  ◼  N  A  A  F  ◼  ◼
```

CONNECT THE DOTS: HOSTILE MOB

Connect the dots to discover the original boss Mob!

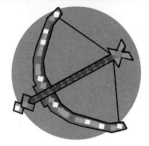

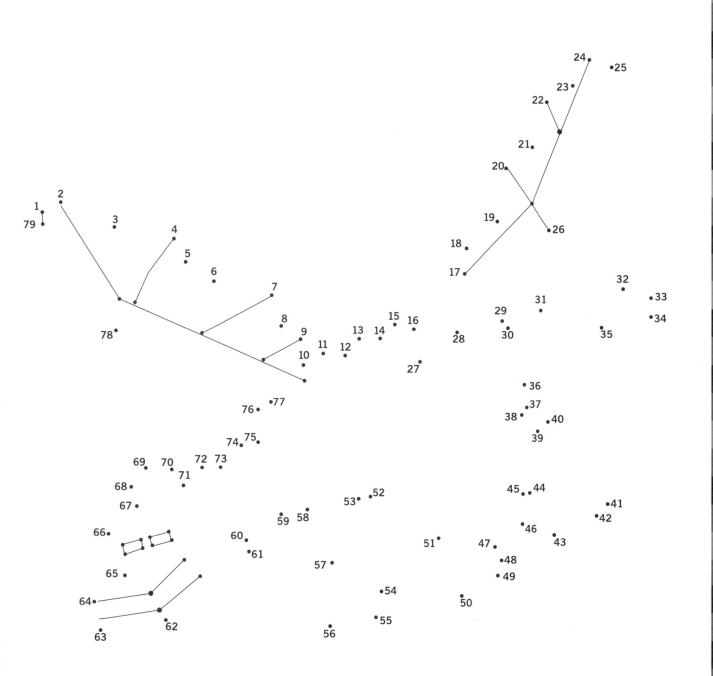

MIXED UP

Write the answers to the clues on the spaces, one letter on each blank. Then transfer the letters to the boxes below that have the same numbers. If you fill in the boxes correctly, you'll reveal something Alex loves to brew.

Big smile
$\overline{}_{9}\ \overline{}_{6}\ \overline{}_{13}\ \overline{}_{3}$

12 o'clock p.m.
$\overline{}_{15}\ \overline{}_{11}\ \overline{}_{14}\ \overline{}_{8}$

Pork chop source
$\overline{}_{10}\ \overline{}_{2}\ \overline{}_{4}$

Ceramic square on a bathroom floor
$\overline{}_{12}\ \overline{}_{7}\ \overline{}_{1}\ \overline{}_{5}$

1	2	3	4	5	6	7	8	9

10	11	12	13	14	15

A SMALL PROBLEM

Every word in Column B contains the same letters as a word in Column A, plus one extra letter. Draw a line between word "matches," then write the extra letter on the space provided.

Unscramble the column of letters to reveal a small problem for Minecrafters.

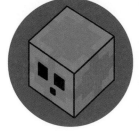

Column A	Column B	
Drips	Slime	M
Wasp	Tamed	__
Lies	Spider	__
Unreal	Hostile	__
Thaw	Neutral	__
Hotels	Pearl	__
Meat	Wheat	__
Trace	Spawn	__
Leap	Create	__

__ __ __ __ __ __ __ __ __

CRACK THE CODE

You don't need a pickaxe to crack this code, just your brain.

Use the code below to find the answer to the joke:

Why did Steve attack the cake with a stick?

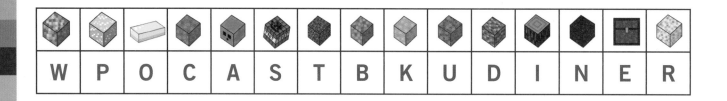

W	P	O	C	A	S	T	B	K	U	D	I	N	E	R

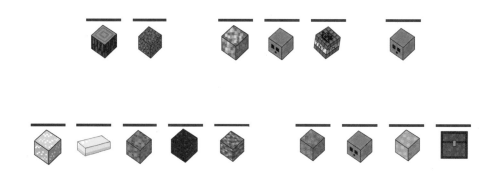

34

ALPHA CODE

The answer to the joke will be revealed as you add letters to the empty boxes that come before, between, or after the given letters in the alphabet. If you get to Z, start all over again with A. The first letter has already been written for you.

Why was the Ender Dragon book a flop?

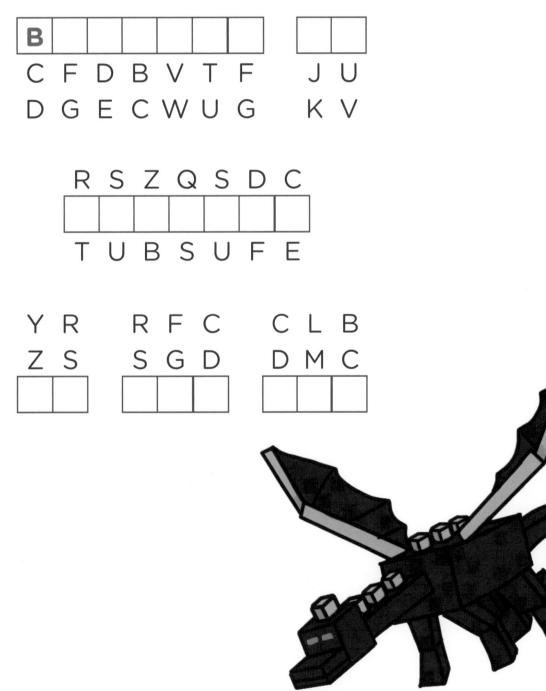

| **B** | | | | | | | | | |

C F D B V T F   J U
D G E C W U G   K V

R S Z Q S D C

T U B S U F E

Y R   R F C   C L B
Z S   S G D   D M C

GRAB AND GO CHALLENGE

Pick up every single experience orb in this maze, but do it quickly to escape the zombie chasing you. You'll need to draw a line from Start to Stop that passes through every orb once. Your line can go up, down, left, or right, but not diagonally. On your mark, get set, go!

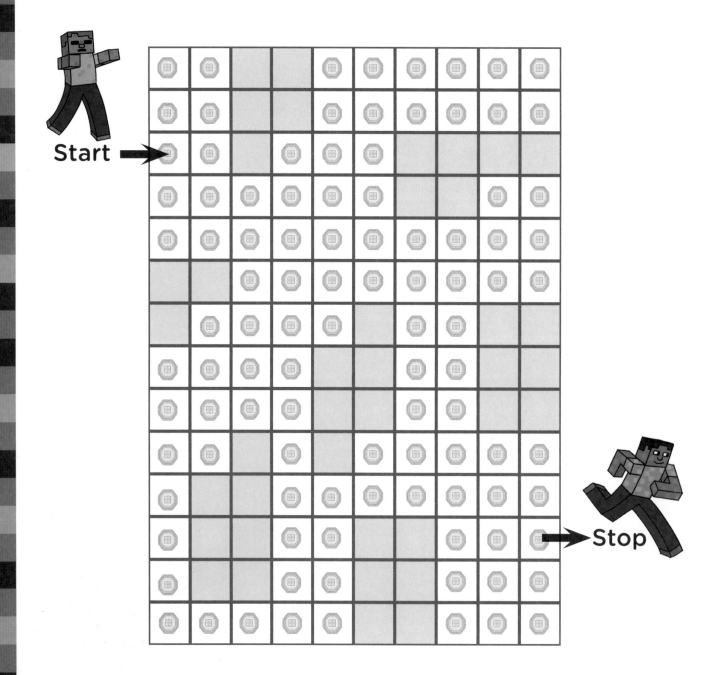

Start →

→ Stop

WORD MINE

Find and circle the names of fourteen raw materials in the wordfind. They might be forward, backward, up, down, or diagonal. Watch out! Every R, A, and W has been replaced with a redstone block.

BLAZE ROD
DIAMOND
DRAGON'S BREATH
ENDER PEARL
FEATHER
FLINT
GLOWSTONE DUST
GOLD INGOT
LEATHER
MAGMA CREAM
NETHER WART
PRISMARINE SHARD
REDSTONE
STRING

B		G		F	N	F	X	D	I		M	O	N	D
I	E	H	T		E		B	S	N	O	G			D
E	H	J	E		T	H	O	G	U	M	E	X	C	T
N	T	D	T	N	H	E	N	P		L	N		B	O
D		H	L	U	E	I	N	E	I	B	G	L	O	G
E	E	M		Z		K		O	P	M		D	H	N
	L	O	C	T		C	T	F	T	Z	L	L	E	I
P		I	S	M			I	N	E	S	H			D
E	Z	E	G	M		T	I		I	H	D	O	F	L
	U	N	G	O	T	M	O	B	S	L	Z	E	I	O
	P		S	D	K	D	U	J		T	F	I		G
L	M	G	L	O		S	T	O	N	E	D	U	S	T

CIRCLE OF TRUTH: FUN FACT

Start at the ▼ *. Write every third letter on the spaces to reveal a Minecrafting secret.*

▼

Y_ _ _ _ _ _ _ , _ _ _ _ _ _ _ _ _ _ _ _ _

_ _ _ _ _ _ _ _ _ _ _ _

ZOMBIE TWINS

Only two of these zombies are exactly the same. Which two are identical?

CAN YOU DIG IT?

Turn MINE into ORES one letter at a time. The answer to each clue looks like the word above it, except one letter is different. If you get stuck, try working from the bottom up.

| M | I | N | E |

A silent actor

Ten-cent coin

Darkens slowly

Points at a target

Where elbows are found

Greek god of war

| O | R | E | S |

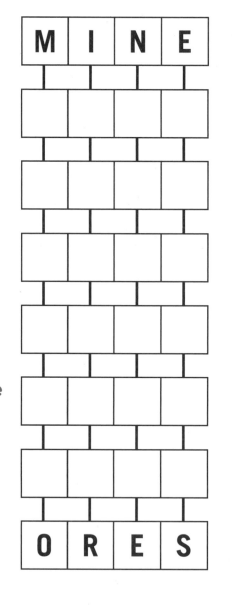

SQUARED UP: FARM MOBS

Each of the four Mobs in this puzzle can appear only once in each row, each column, and the four inside boxes. Fill in the remaining empty boxes with the first letter of a Mob shown below.

C = COW   P = PIG   H = HORSE   S = SHEEP

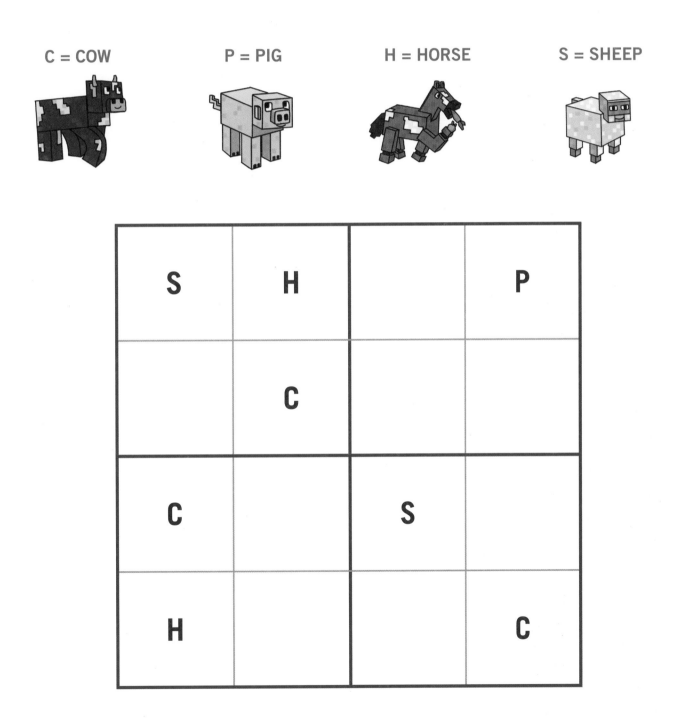

GROW WITH THE FLOW

Find the flow of letters that spell out a fun fact for Minecrafters. Start with the corner letter, then read every third letter, moving clockwise around the square, until all the letters are used.

Start

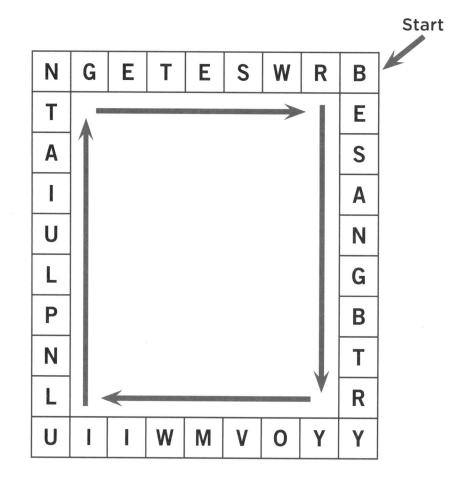

N	G	E	T	E	S	W	R	B
T								E
A								S
I								A
U								N
L								G
P								B
N								T
L								R
U	I	I	W	M	V	O	Y	Y

‒ ‒ ‒ ‒ ‒ ‒   ‒ ‒ ‒ ‒ ‒ ‒ ‒ ‒ ‒   ‒ ‒ ‒ ‒   ‒ ‒

‒ ‒ ‒ ‒ ‒ ‒   ‒ ‒ ‒ ‒ ‒ ‒ ‒

BASIC TRAINING

Boxes connected by lines contain the same letter. Some letters are given; others have to be guessed. Fill in all the boxes to reveal a list of items with a connection. Do you know what the connection is?

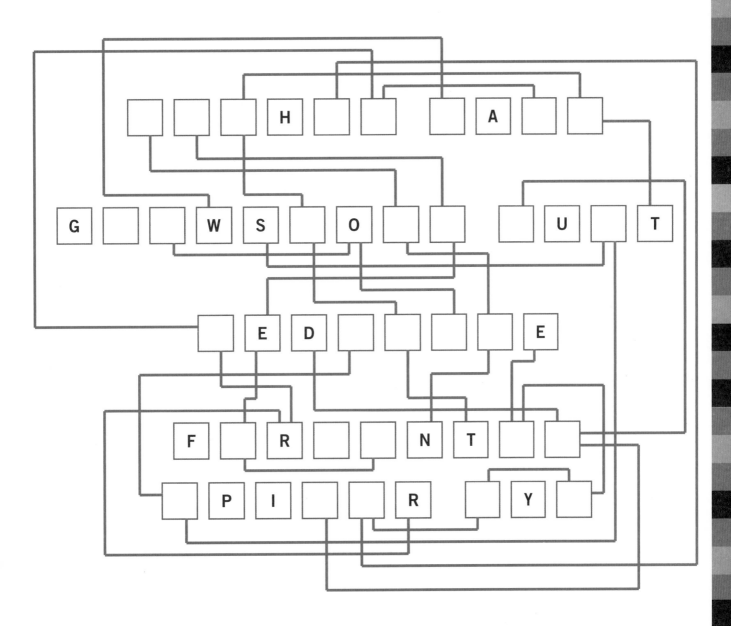

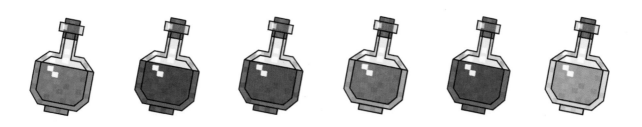

YOU CAN DRAW IT: VILLAGERS

Use the grid to copy the picture. Examine each small square in the top grid, then transfer those lines to the corresponding square in the bottom grid.

THE SHAPE OF THINGS TO COME

Find the six puzzle pieces that fit the shapes in the rectangle. Watch out! Pieces might be rotated or flipped and not all of them will be used. Write the letters of the correct pieces on the spaces below to answer the question:

What Mob helps keep creepers away?

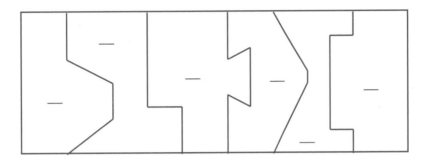

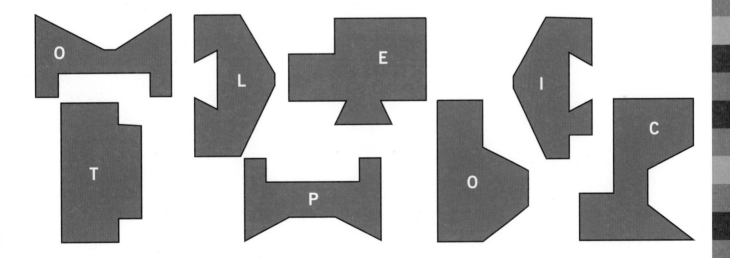

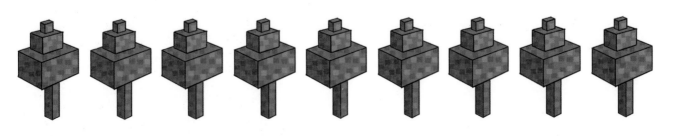

WHEN PIGS HIDE

This pigsty contains thirteen hidden pigs. Can you find them all?

MINER'S BLOCK

Find and circle the names of eight gems in the wordfind below. They might be forward, backward, up, down, or diagonal. Write unused letters on the spaces, in order from top to bottom and left to right, to uncover a tip for mining.

Hint: Circle individual letters instead of the whole word at once. The first one has been done for you.

COAL   EMERALD   IRON   NETHER QUARTZ

DIAMOND   GOLD   LAPIS LAZULI REDSTONE

```
R   D   D   I   L   G   A   D   R   O   U   N
E   I   L   U   Z   A   L   S   I   P   A   L
D   D   O   D   I   A   O   A   M   O   N   I
S   D   G   O   R   R   E   C   S   O   R   D
T   I   A   E   M   D   I   A   M   O   N   D
O   O   M   N   D   S   D   O   N   N   T   F
N   E   T   H   E   R   Q   U   A   R   T   Z
E   A   L   L   I   N   T   O   L   A   V   A
```

__ __ __ __ __ __ __ __ __ __ __ __ __ __ __

__ __ __ __ __ __ __ __ __ __ __ __ __ ,

__ __ __ __ __ __ __ __ __ __ __ __ __ __ __ .

TRUE OR FALSE?

Find your way through this maze from Start to Finish. It will be easier if you answer the questions correctly!

Start

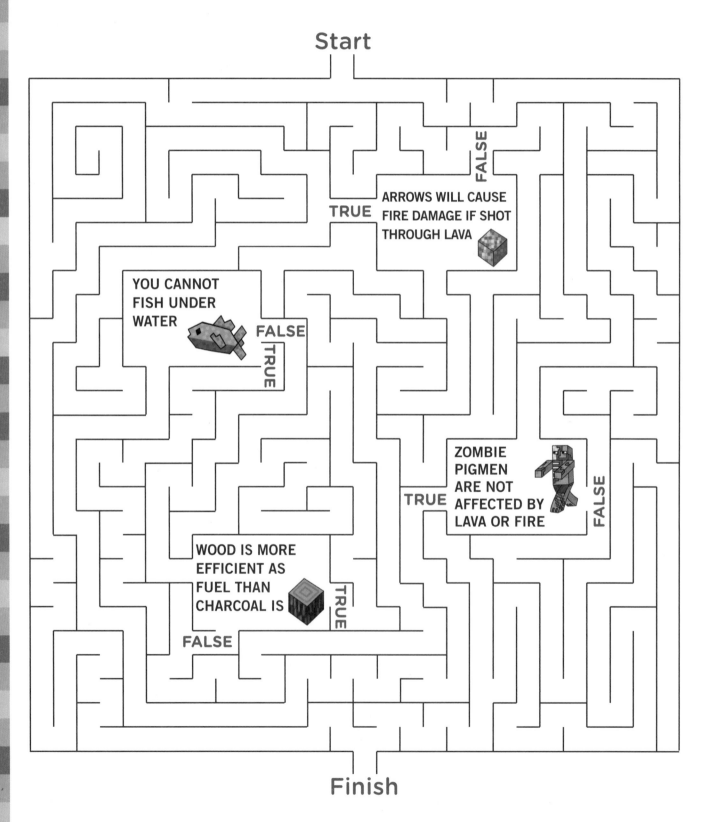

FALSE

TRUE — ARROWS WILL CAUSE FIRE DAMAGE IF SHOT THROUGH LAVA

YOU CANNOT FISH UNDER WATER

FALSE
TRUE

ZOMBIE PIGMEN ARE NOT AFFECTED BY LAVA OR FIRE

TRUE

FALSE

WOOD IS MORE EFFICIENT AS FUEL THAN CHARCOAL IS

TRUE

FALSE

Finish

STEVE SAYS: JOKE TIME

Reveal the answer to the joke by doing what Steve says—and only what Steve says!

	1	2	3	4	5
A	ONE	CRACKS	HEALING	ALL	STRENGTH
B	418	IF	THIRTEEN	WAX	LEAPING
C	ROADS	HISS	ARE	A	BOOM
D	HACKS	THIRTY	INVISIBILITY	ON	7,359,864
E	RATTLE	BLOCKED	MOAN	IT	SWIFTNESS

1. Steve says, "Cross off all numbers in Rows B and D and Column 1."

2. Steve says, "Cross off all potions in Columns in 3 and 5."

3. Steve says, "Cross off words that rhyme with 'axe.'"

4. Cross off words that start or end with vowels.

5. Steve says, "Cross off all Mob sounds in Rows C and E."

6. Steve says, "Cross off words with fewer than three letters in Columns 2 and 4."

7. Steve says, "Write the remaining four words to reveal the answer to the joke."

Why are there no cars in Minecraft?

_____   _____   _____   _____

ON THE PLAYGROUND

Take a good look to find the ten differences between these two pictures.

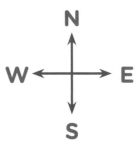

ENCHANTED MAP

This End City map is enchanted. To reveal its contents, you must press all twelve buttons in the right order and land on the F button last. Use the letters and numbers on the buttons to direct you.

Which button must you push first to get to F last?

Hint: 1N means press the button one space north; 2E means move two spaces east. W=west and S=south.

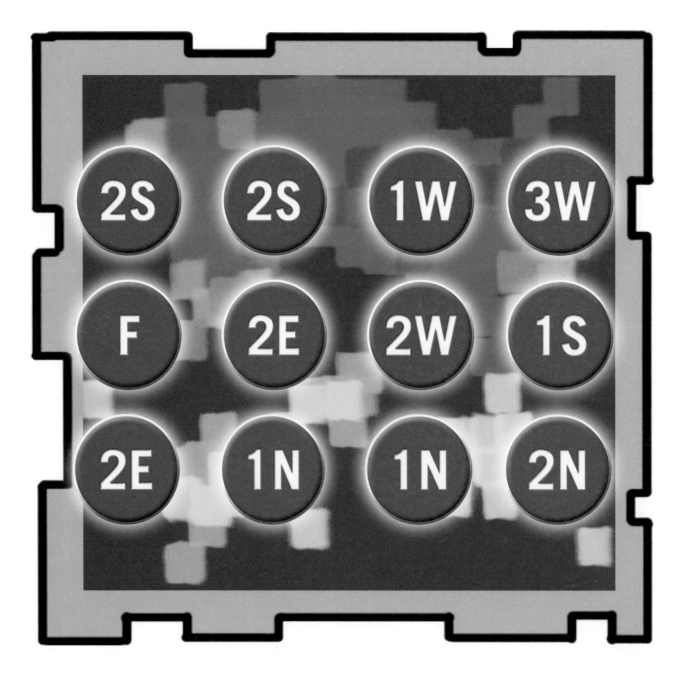

COMMON CODE

Use the key to identify three items that are familiar to Minecrafters. Then use the key to fill in the last set of blank spaces to reveal where all three items are found.

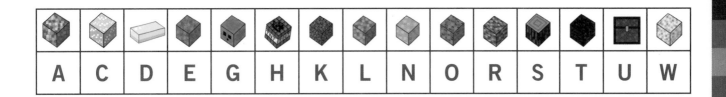

A	C	D	E	G	H	K	L	N	O	R	S	T	U	W

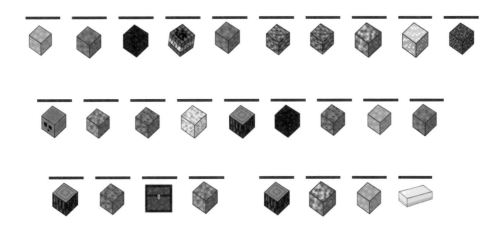

What do the three words above have in common?

They're all found in

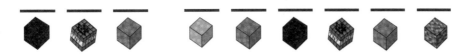

EVERY NOOK AND CRANNY

Draw a line from Start to Stop that passes through every apple once and only once. Your line can go up, down, left, or right, but not diagonally. On your mark, get set, go!

Start

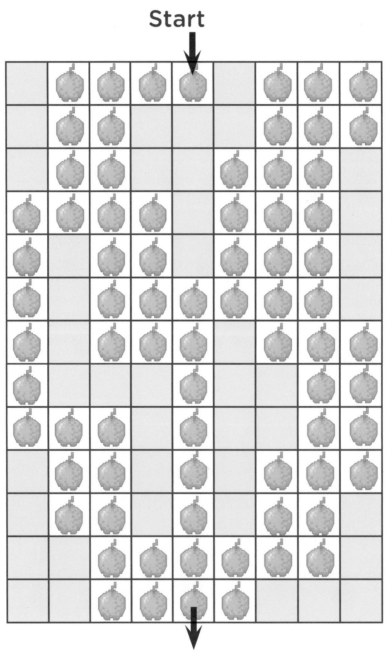

Stop

CIRCLE OF TRUTH: SURVIVAL TIP

Start at the ⬇ *. Write every third letter on the spaces to reveal a truth about Minecraft.*

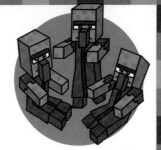

W _ ,

_ _ _ _ _ _ _ _ _ _ _ _ _ _ _ _ _ _

SKELETON TWINS

Only two of these skeletons are exactly the same. Which two are identical? Circle the twins.

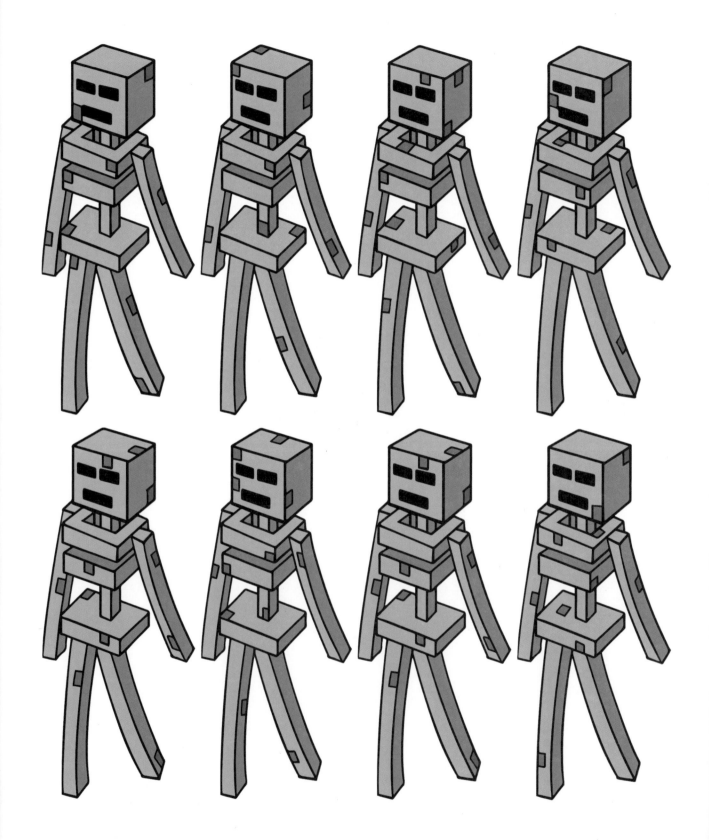

CONNECT THE DOTS: PIT OF PERIL!

Connect the dots to complete this perilous scene.

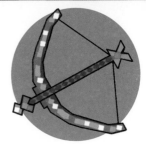

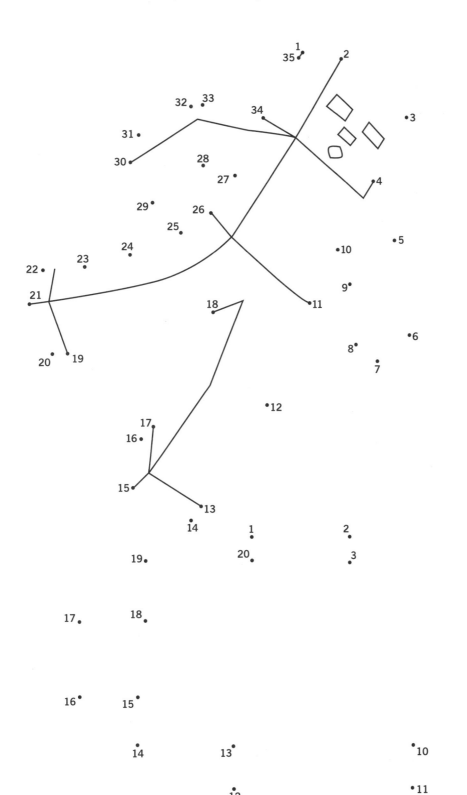

SQUARED UP: BLOCK PARTY

Each of the six blocks in this puzzle can appear only once in each row, each column, and pink rectangle. Use the letter C to represent a clay block, the letter D for a dirt block, and so on. Can you fill every square with the right letter?

C = Clay   **D = Dirt**   **G = Gravel**   **I = Ice**   **O = Obsidian**   **S = Sand**

	I	G	C	O	
O	C			G	I
I		S	D		G
D		C	O		S
C	S			D	O
	D	O	I	S	

HOLD IT!

It's time to discuss a weighty matter. Start with the corner letter, then read every third letter, moving clockwise around the square, and write them in the blank spaces below until you solve the mystery message.

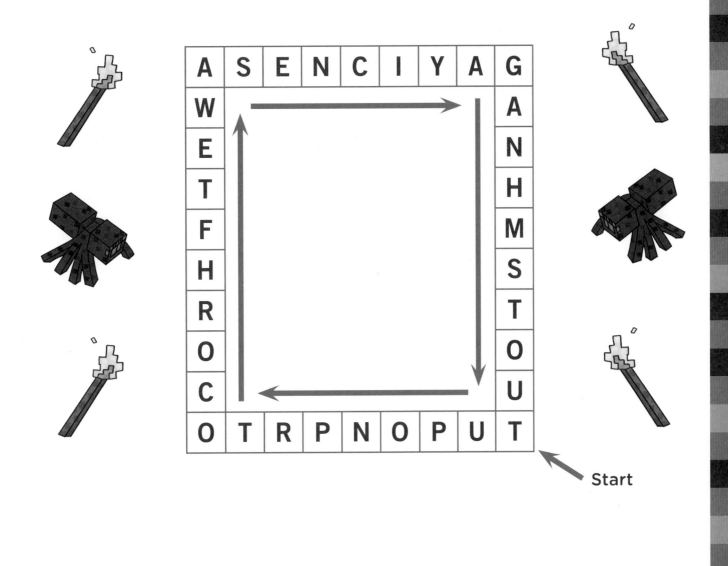

Start

COLLECTING TREASURE

Four treasures are yours for the taking—and you want them all! Find the path that allows you to collect the four treasures between Start and Finish. Heads up! Paths go under and over each other.

Start

Finish

CIRCLE OF TRUTH: FOOD FOR THOUGHT

Start at the ⬇ *.*

Write every third letter on the spaces to reveal a Minecrafting secret.

E H C A U A T N U I G S N E E G R S P A P U N O F I D F N S E A O R U N F S I I E N S A G H

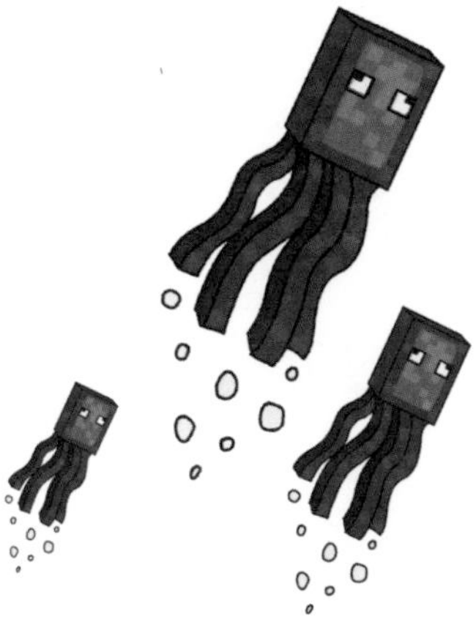

E _ _ _ _ _   _ _ _ _ _ _ _ _ _ _

_ _ _ _ _ _   _ _ _ _ _ _ _ _ _ _,

_ _ _ _ _ _, _ _ _   _ _ _ _ _ _ _

YOU CAN DRAW IT: IRON GOLEM

Use the grid to copy the picture. Examine the lines in each small square in the grid at the left, then transfer those lines to the corresponding square in the grid on the right.

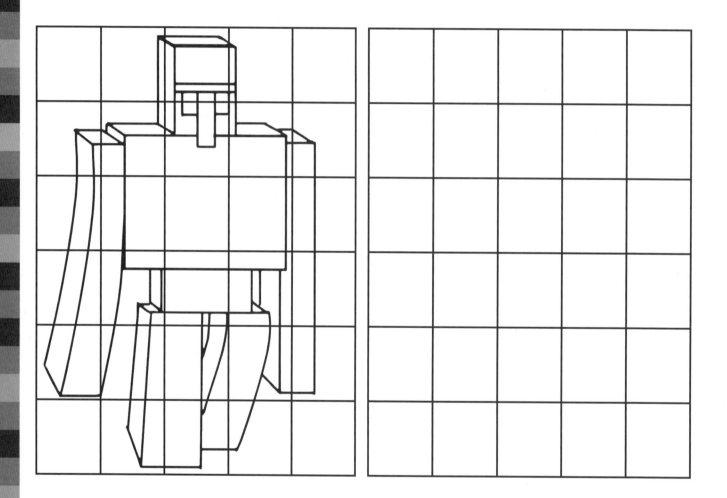

TIP FOR ENDING ENDERMEN

Step 1: Find the ten puzzle pieces that fit the shapes in the rectangle. Watch out! Pieces might be rotated or flipped. Write the letters of the correct pieces on the spaces. Not all pieces are used below.

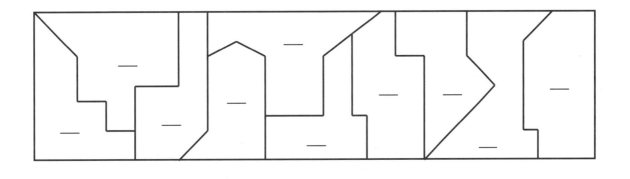

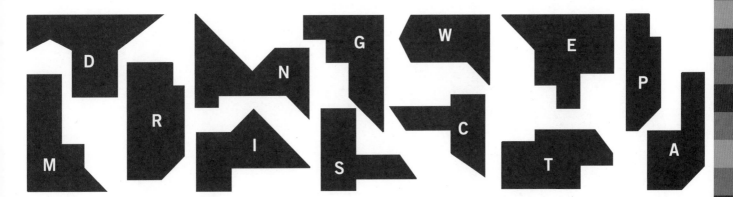

Step 2: Write the letters from the spaces above in the boxes that have the same numbers to reveal something that can help you destroy Endermen.

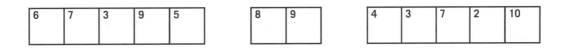

WORD FARM

The words bat, cow, pig, sheep, spider, squid, chicken, rabbit, donkey, horse, mule, polar bear, ocelot, *and* wolf *are hiding on this farm. How many words can you spot?*

CONNECT THE DOTS: FARM LIFE

Connect the dots to to see what's happening on the Minecrafter's farm.

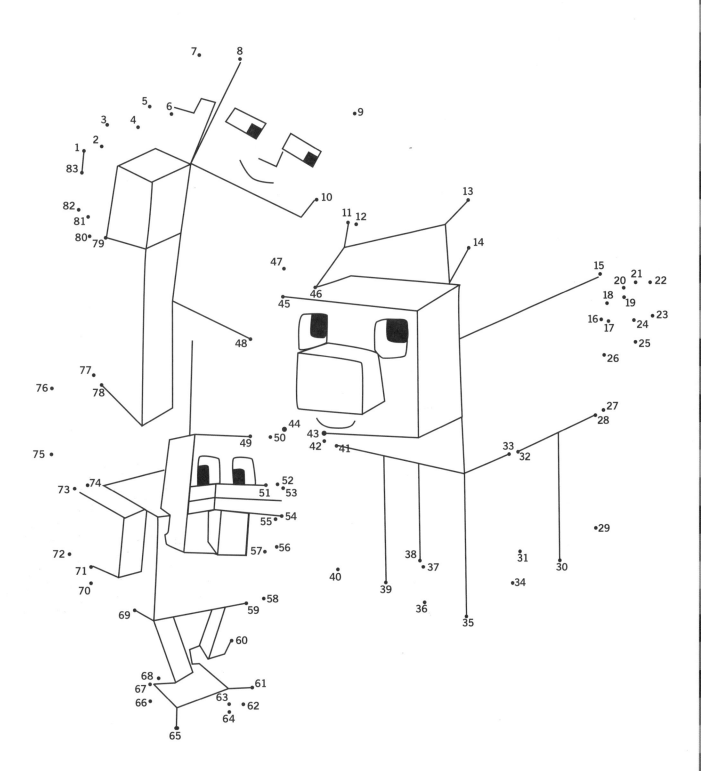

HUNT FOR ENCHANTMENTS

Find and circle the names of fifteen enchantments in the wordfind below. They might be forward, backward, up, down, or diagonal. Write unused letters on the blank spaces, in order from top to bottom and left to right, to discover a fun fact about enchantments.

Hint: Circle individual letters instead of whole words. We've found one to get you started.

```
H  O  O  K  C  A  B  K  C  O  N  K
E  F  F  I  C  I  E  N  C  Y  K  M
P  O  I  S  M  I  T  E  R  S  I  G
R  E  F  R  I  S  N  H  H  W  N  N
O  E  G  I  E  U  T  A  H  I  F  I
T  M  T  N  T  A  R  H  K  E  I  D
E  A  P  R  I  P  S  A  L  P  N  N
C  L  O  O  N  T  E  P  U  U  I  E
T  F  R  E  W  R  O  E  E  N  T  M
I  E  S  N  B  E  C  O  H  C  Y  A
O  S  N  N  T  M  R  E  L  H  T  N
N  T  U  S  I  L  K  T  O  U  C  H
```

EFFICIENCY
FIRE ASPECT
FLAME
FORTUNE
INFINITY
KNOCKBACK
~~LOOTING~~
MENDING
POWER
PROTECTION
PUNCH
SHARPNESS
SILK TOUCH
SMITE
UNBREAKING

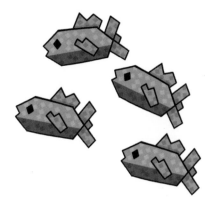

___ ___ ___ ___   ___ ___ ___ ___   ___ ___ ___ ___   ___ ___ ___

___ ___ ___   ___ ___ ___ ___   ___ ___ ___ ___

ROTTEN LUCK

Take your chances with this dangerous maze and avoid food poisoning at all costs. Choose a path from the Start box. There's only one lucky path that leads to a quiet corner and a delicious cookie. The rest lead to the dreaded rotten flesh! Good luck!

Start

YOU WIN!

BAD LUCK AHEAD!

TURN BACK!

DANGER

MULTIPLAYER MISMATCH

These two pictures are nearly identical, except for ten little differences.
How many of these differences can you find?

TWIN MOBS

Only two of these villagers are exactly the same.
Which two are identical?

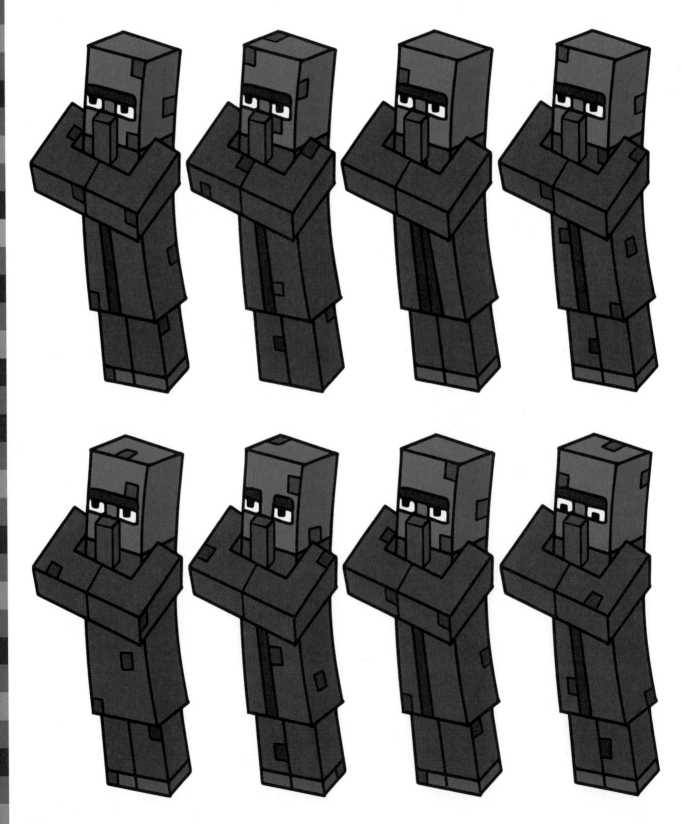

PATH OF DOOM

Begin at the dot below each player's name and work your way down to figure out how each player met their doom. Every time you hit a horizontal line (one that goes across), you must follow it.

Which player was destroyed by an exploding creeper?

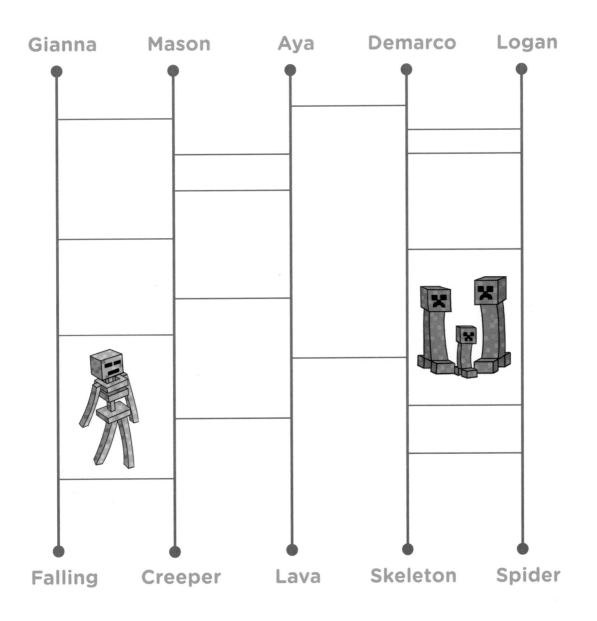

Gianna   Mason   Aya   Demarco   Logan

Falling   Creeper   Lava   Skeleton   Spider

TRUTH OR TALE?

This is a two-part puzzle. First, name the icons and figure out where each word goes in the crossword. Use the arrows to help you place the first two words. Second, transfer the numbered letters from the crossword to the numbered spaces at the bottom to reveal a claim about Minecraft.

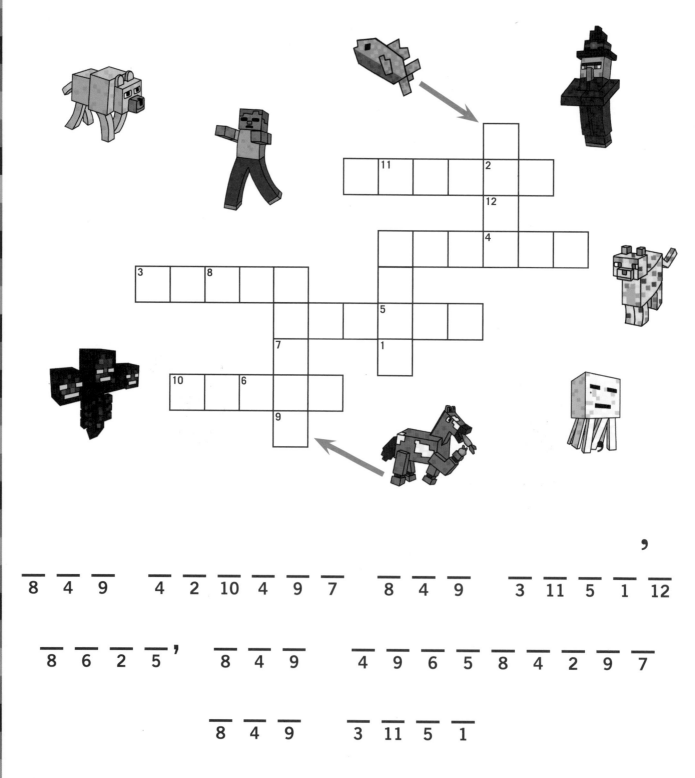

,

$\overline{8}$ $\overline{4}$ $\overline{9}$ $\overline{4}$ $\overline{2}$ $\overline{10}$ $\overline{4}$ $\overline{9}$ $\overline{7}$ $\overline{8}$ $\overline{4}$ $\overline{9}$ $\overline{3}$ $\overline{11}$ $\overline{5}$ $\overline{1}$ $\overline{12}$

$\overline{8}$ $\overline{6}$ $\overline{2}$ $\overline{5}$, $\overline{8}$ $\overline{4}$ $\overline{9}$ $\overline{4}$ $\overline{9}$ $\overline{6}$ $\overline{5}$ $\overline{8}$ $\overline{4}$ $\overline{2}$ $\overline{9}$ $\overline{7}$

$\overline{8}$ $\overline{4}$ $\overline{9}$ $\overline{3}$ $\overline{11}$ $\overline{5}$ $\overline{1}$

CONNECT THE DOTS: OUR HERO

Connect the dots and find out who always saves the day.

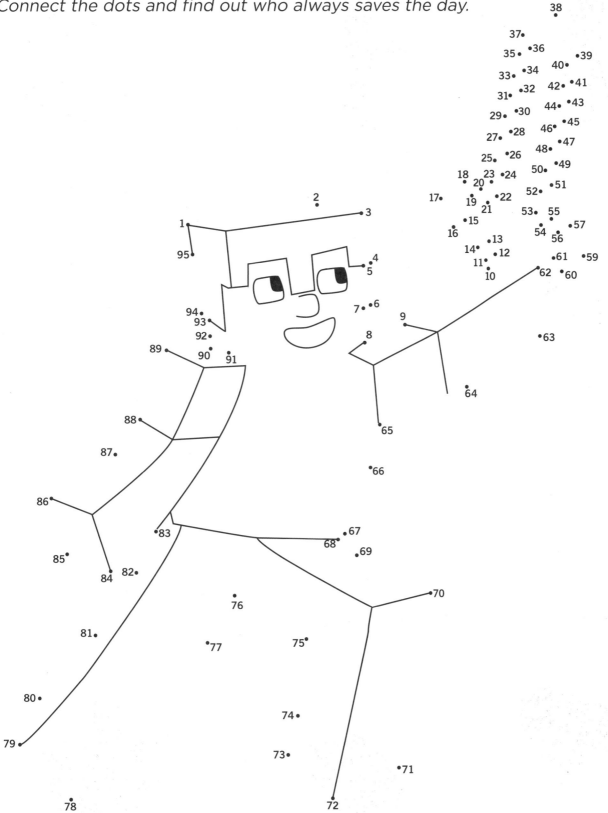

TERMS OF THE GAME

Use the clues (not the pictures this time) to find words that fit in the boxes below.

ACROSS

3 Come to life in the game world

5 An object that is fired at

8 The hunger bar is visible in this mode

9 Begin fighting with

12 Brew potions or power lights with this

15 A C O U R S E E R pack allows players to customize textures, sounds, and more *(Unscramble the word on the space)*

16 This plus cocoa beans makes a cookie

17 Default game character

18 Forest or desert, for example

DOWN

1 Leafless desert plant, often with sharp spikes

2 Entryway to another world

4 Use this to make paper

6 Biome with sand dunes, dead bushes, and cacti

7 Where skin and tools are displayed

10 This type of Mob runs away when hurt

11 Builder's favorite mode

13 Have lava flow on top of water to create this

14 Lava sources and random fires are hazards here

SQUARED UP: INVENTORY

Each of the six inventory items in this puzzle can appear only once in each row, each column, and pink rectangle. Use the letter A to represent apple, the letter C for carrot, and so on. Can you fill every block with the proper item?

 A = Apple   C = Carrot   M = Milk   P = Potion   S = Sword   W = Wheat

W	S	P	C	M	
M		A			P
P				C	
C	M		A	P	S
S			P		M
	P	M		W	

Your mission is find the fact in the letters below. Start with a letter in one of the corners (you have to figure out which one), then read every third letter, going clockwise around the square, until all of the letters are used.

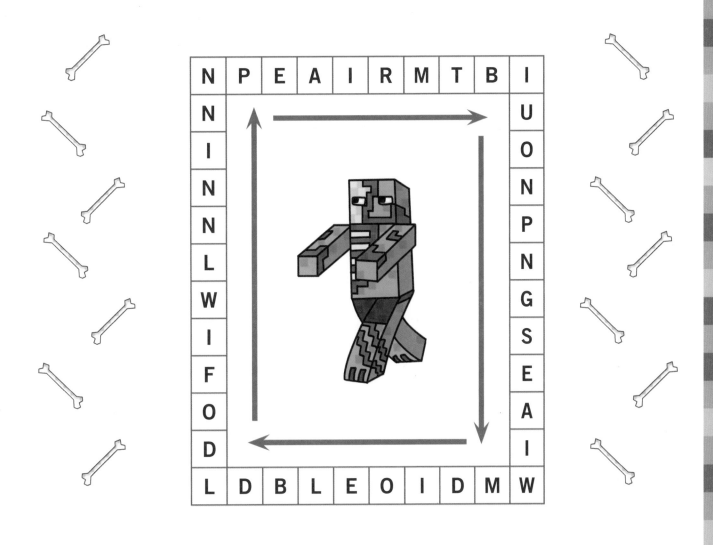

N	P	E	A	I	R	M	T	B	I
N									U
I									O
N									N
N									P
L									N
W									G
I									S
F									E
O									A
D									I
L	D	B	L	E	O	I	D	M	W

" _ _ _ _ _ _ _   _ _ _ _ _ _ "

_ _ _ _ _ _ _ _ _ _ _ _ _ _ _

BLACKOUT

Read the clues and write the answers across the blank boxes. If you need help, the answers are scrambled around the border.

When all the boxes are full, read the vertical shaded boxes to answer this question:

Which potion is helpful when exploring the Nether and the ocean?

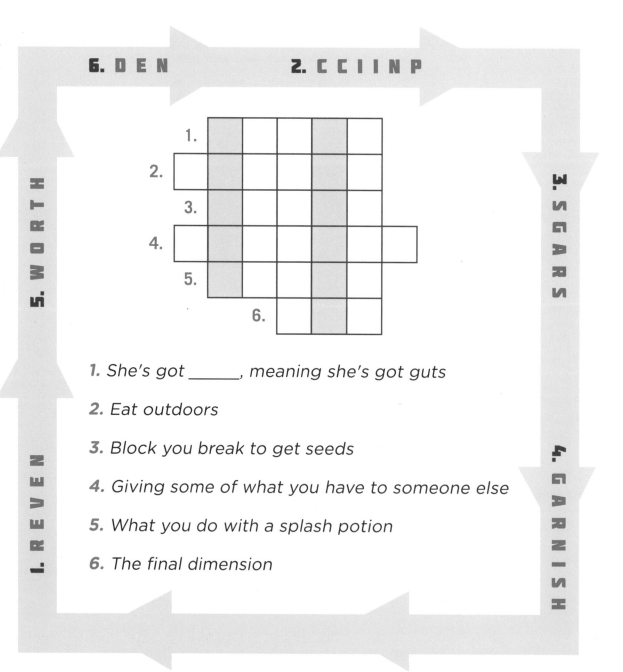

6. D E N

2. C C I I N P

3. S G A R S

5. W O R T H

1. R E V E N

4. G A R N I S H

1. She's got _____, meaning she's got guts

2. Eat outdoors

3. Block you break to get seeds

4. Giving some of what you have to someone else

5. What you do with a splash potion

6. The final dimension

MULTIPLAYER CTM CHALLENGE

Four friends are collecting hardened clay blocks to Complete the Monument.

Which player collected yellow blocks?

To find out, begin at the dot below each player's name and follow it downward. Every time you hit a horizontal line (one that goes across), you must take it. See where each player's path leads.

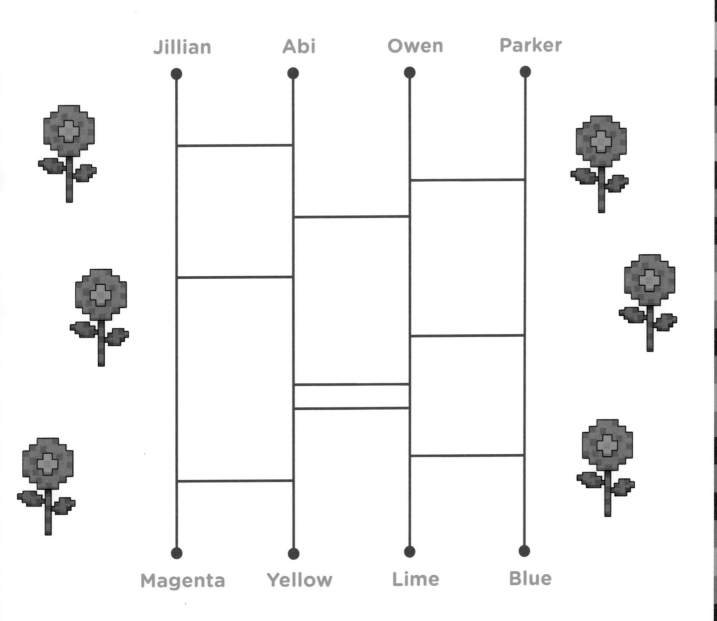

HERE, THERE, AND EVERYWHERE

In your search for dropped treasure, you must visit every nook and cranny in this maze before nightfall. Draw a line from Start to Stop that passes through every gold ingot once—and only once. Your line can go up, down, left, or right, but not diagonally. On your mark, get set, go!

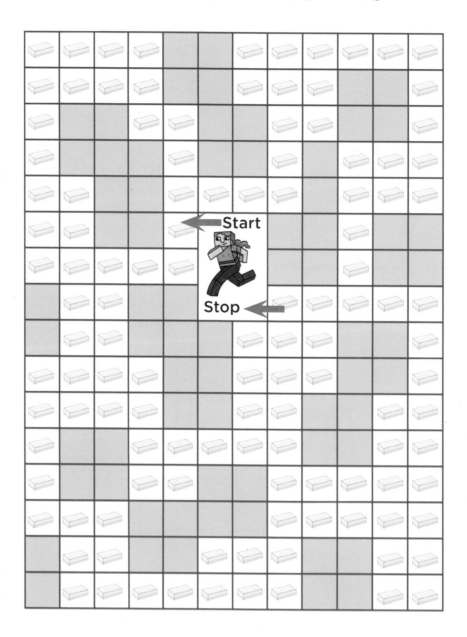

DEFLECT THIS

Every word in Column B contains the same letters as a word in Column A, plus one letter. Draw a line between each pair of "matching" words, then write the extra letter on the space provided. Unscramble the column of letters to reveal something you might want to deflect . . . or not.

COLUMN A	COLUMN B	EXTRA LETTER
Tinge	Bedrock	__
Dread	Wander	__
Meal	Damage	__
Verse	Smelt	__
Drawn	Ladder	__
Corked	Ignite	I
Stem	Flame	__
Gamed	Server	__

__ __ __ __ __ __ __

DOWN ON THE (MOB) FARM

The answer to each clue looks like the word above it, except one letter is different. If you get stuck, try working from the bottom up.

	F	A	R	M

Damage

Close relative of the rabbit

Female horse

Fourth planet from the sun

Bulk or size

Green plant that grows in moist places

	M	O	B	S

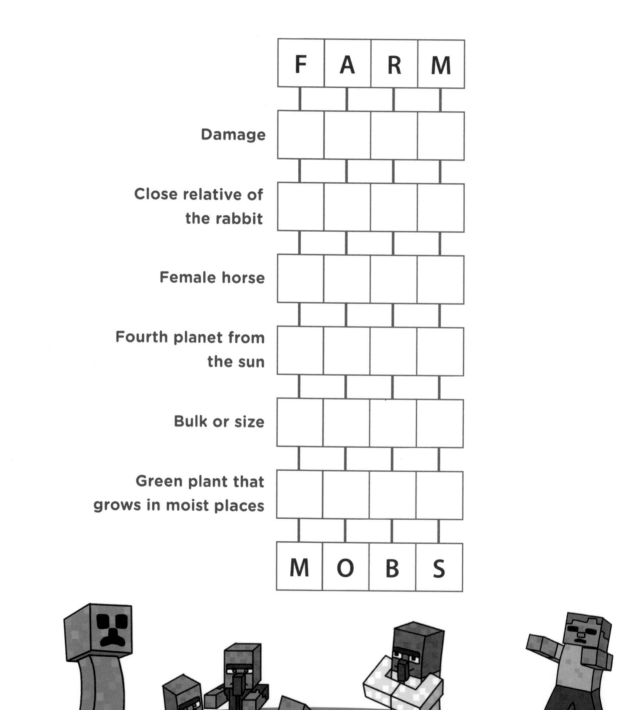

PLACES, PEOPLE!

Use the clues to determine where each of the nine Mobs goes in the three-by-three grid. Write the name of each Mob in pencil inside the box where you think it belongs.

Snow Golem

Zombie Pigman

Pig

Skeleton

Wolf

Slime

Villager

Spider

Sheep

1. All Mob names that begin with S are in the bottom two rows.

2. The pumpkin-headed Mob is in the center box.

3. The Mob that can be tamed is in a top corner.

4. The zombie and the eight-legged Mob are side-by-side in the bottom row.

5. The two farm animals are stacked one on top of the other in the top right.

6. The Mob in the bottom center box was a pig who got struck by lightning.

7. The arrow-shooting Mob is in a corner.

8. The Mob in the top center box might be a blacksmith or a librarian.

83

CERTIFICATE OF ACHIEVEMENT
CONGRATULATIONS

This certifies that

_____

became a

MINECRAFT PUZZLE BOSS

on _____.

Date

_____

Signature

ANSWERS

GOING BATTY

STEVE SAYS...

CREEPERS WERE THE RESULT OF A CODING MISTAKE

(What was supposed to be a pig wound up with extra-long legs, and the result turned into a creeper.)

THE MIRROR'S IMAGE

ENDERMEN WERE CALLED "FARLANDERS" BEFORE THE END WAS CREATED

CITY SLICKER

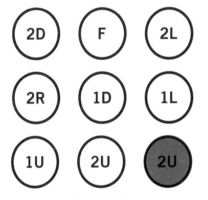

TAKE A GUESS

EXIT, CORN, PINE, SEEP

EXPERIENCE POINTS

ENCHANTED CHEST

(2D)	(F)	(2L)
(2R)	(1D)	(1L)
(1U)	(2U)	(2U)

The red button is the first one pressed.

SEE AND SOLVE

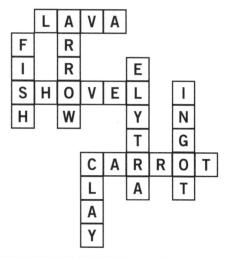

THEY FIRE EVERYONE

HOME SWEET BIOME

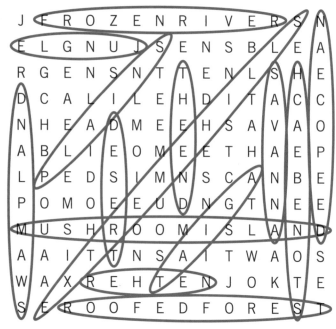

CREEPER TWINS

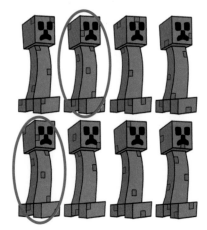

CIRCLE OF TRUTH: CRAFTING CLUE

*DIAMOND MAKES THE
STRONGEST TOOLS*

MOB SCENE

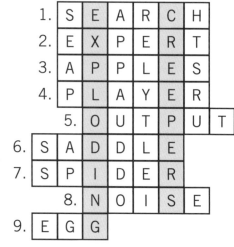

1. S E A R C H
2. E X P E R T
3. A P P L E S
4. P L A Y E R
5. O U T P U T
6. S A D D L E
7. S P I D E R
8. N O I S E
9. E G G

EXPLODING CREEPERS

SQUARED UP:
MOBS IN EVERY QUARTER

G	C	S	B
B	S	G	C
C	G	B	S
S	B	C	G

WATCHTOWER QUEST

A CURE FOR WHAT AILS YOU

DRINKING A BUCKET OF MILK CURES POISONING

PIECE IT TOGETHER

W _ I _ T _ H _ E _ R _ S

PICK, THE RIGHT TOOL!

TOOL CHEST

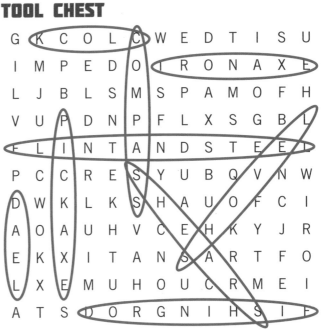

```
G K C O L C W E D T I S U
I M P E D O I R O N A X E
L J B L S M S P A M O F H
V U P D N P F L X S G B L
F L I N T A N D S T E E L
P C C R E S Y U B Q V N W
D W K L K S H A U O F C I
A O A U H V C E H K Y J R
E K X I T A N S A R T F O
L X E M U H O U C R M E I
A T S D O R G N I H S I F
```

FIND THE PORTAL

Zombie94   Shtomp   Enchantress56   Gash

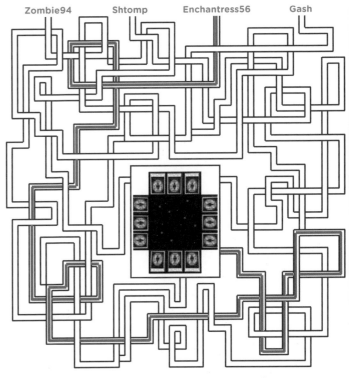

Enchantress56 finds the portal.

87

CROSSWORD CLUE FINDER

SURVIVAL MAZE

SEE THE SEA

BLOCKED!

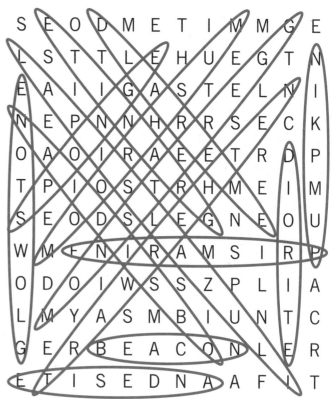

POWER PLAY: MYSTERY WORD

REDSTONE

CONNECT THE DOTS: HOSTILE MOB

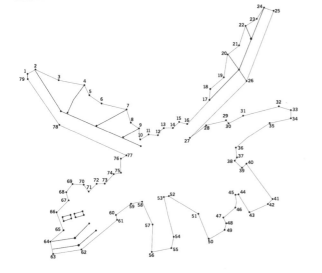

MIXED UP

GRIN, NOON, PIG, TILE
LINGERING POTION

A SMALL PROBLEM

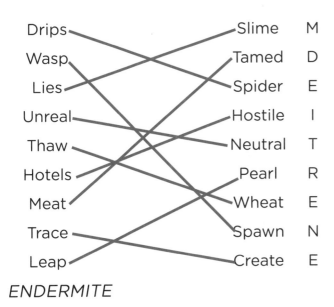

Column A	Column B	
Drips	Slime	M
Wasp	Tamed	D
Lies	Spider	E
Unreal	Hostile	I
Thaw	Neutral	T
Hotels	Pearl	R
Meat	Wheat	E
Trace	Spawn	N
Leap	Create	E

ENDERMITE

CRACK THE CODE

IT WAS A POUND CAKE

ALPHA CODE

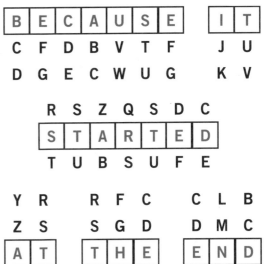

B	E	C	A	U	S	E		I	T
C	F	D	B	V	T	F		J	U
D	G	E	C	W	U	G		K	V

R	S	Z	Q	S	D	C
S	T	A	R	T	E	D
T	U	B	S	U	F	E

Y	R		R	F	C		C	L	B
Z	S		S	G	D		D	M	C
A	T		T	H	E		E	N	D

GRAB AND GO CHALLENGE

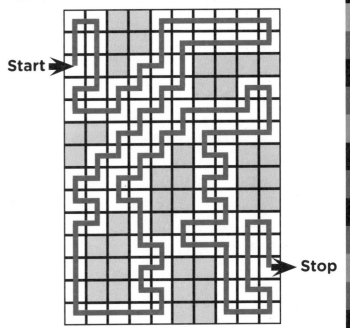

Start ➡

Stop ➡

WORD MINE

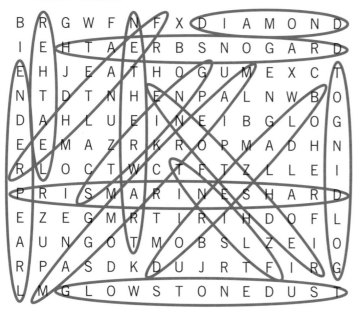

```
B R G W F N F X D I A M O N D
I E H T A E R B S N O G A R D
E H J E A T H O G U M E X C T
N T D T N H E N P A L N W B O
D A H L U E I N E I B G L O G
E E M A Z R K R O P M A D H N
R L O C T W C T F T Z L L E I
P R I S M A R I N E S H A R D
E Z E G M R T I R I H D O F L
A U N G O T M O B S L Z E I O
R P A S D K D U J R T F I R G
L M G L O W S T O N E D U S T
```

CIRCLE OF TRUTH: FUN FACT

YOU CAN'T OPEN A CHEST IF A CAT SITS ON IT

ZOMBIE TWINS

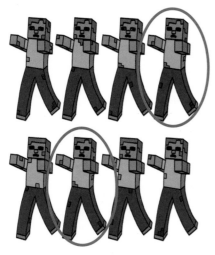

CAN YOU DIG IT?

```
M I N E
M I M E
D I M E
D I M S
A I M S
A R M S
A R E S
O R E S
```

SQUARED UP: FARM MOBS

S	H	C	P
P	C	H	S
C	P	S	H
H	S	P	C

GROW WITH THE FLOW

BABY VILLAGERS GROW UP IN TWENTY MINUTES

You start in the top right corner.

BASIC TRAINING

NETHER WART
GLOWSTONE DUST
REDSTONE
FERMENTED SPIDER EYE
These are the base brewing ingredients.

THE SHAPE OF THINGS TO COME

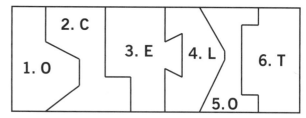

1. O
2. C
3. E
4. L
5. O
6. T

WHEN PIGS HIDE

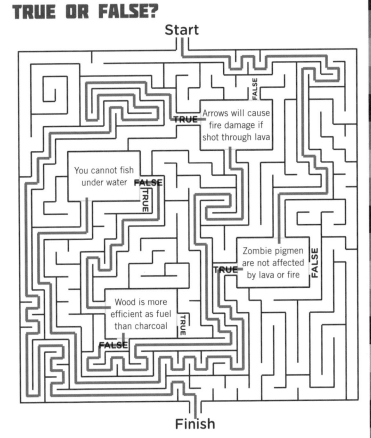

TRUE OR FALSE?

Start

FALSE

TRUE

Arrows will cause
fire damage if
shot through lava

You cannot fish
under water

FALSE

TRUE

Zombie pigmen
are not affected
by lava or fire

FALSE

TRUE

Wood is more
efficient as fuel
than charcoal

TRUE

FALSE

Finish

MINER'S BLOCK

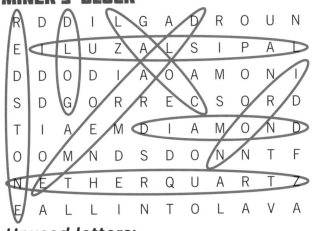

R D D I L G A D R O U N
E I L U Z A L S I P A I
D D O D I A O A M O N I
S D G O R R E C S O R D
T I A E M D I A M O N D
O O M N D S D O N N T F
N E T H E R Q U A R T Z
E A L L I N T O L A V A

Unused letters:

*DIG AROUND DIAMOND ORE
SO DIAMONDS DON'T FALL
INTO LAVA*

STEVE SAYS: JOKE TIME

ALL ROADS ARE BLOCKED

ON THE PLAYGROUND

ENCHANTED MAP

2S	2S	**1W**	3W
F	2E	2W	1S
2E	1N	1N	2N

The red button is the first one pressed.

COMMON CODE

NETHERRACK, GLOWSTONE, SOUL SAND
These things are found only in the Nether

EVERY NOOK AND CRANNY

Start

Stop

CIRCLE OF TRUTH: SURVIVAL TIP

WEAR A PUMPKIN ON YOUR HEAD AND ENDERMEN WON'T GET ANGRY WITH YOU

SKELETON TWINS

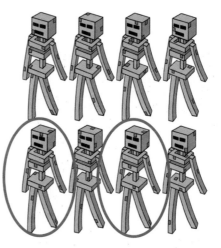

CONNECT THE DOTS: PIT OF PERIL

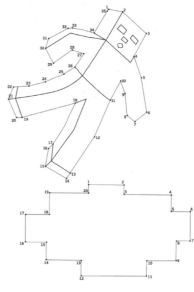

SQUARED UP: BLOCK PARTY

S	I	G	C	O	D
O	C	D	S	G	I
I	O	S	D	C	G
D	G	C	O	I	S
C	S	I	G	D	O
G	D	O	I	S	C

HOLD IT!

TORCHES CAN SUPPORT ANY AMOUNT OF WEIGHT

COLLECTING TREASURE

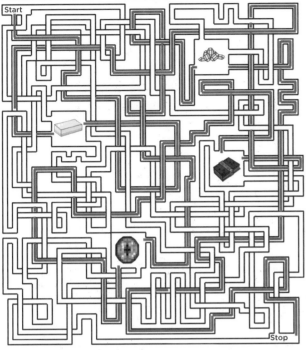

Start

Stop

WORD FARM

CIRCLE OF TRUTH: FOOD FOR THOUGHT

EATING PUFFERFISH CAUSES POISONING, HUNGER, AND NAUSEA

CONNECT THE DOTS: FARM LIFE

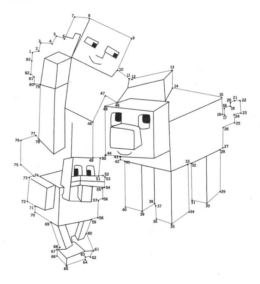

TIP FOR ENDING ENDERMEN

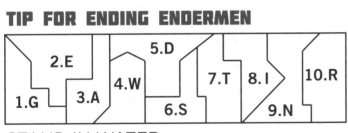

2.E

5.D

4.W

7.T

8.I

10.R

1.G

3.A

6.S

9.N

STAND IN WATER

HUNT FOR ENCHANTMENTS

```
H O O K C A B K C O N K
F F I C I E N C Y K M
P O I S M I T E R S I G
R E F R I S N H H W N N
O E G I E U T A H I F I
T M N T A R H K E I D
E A P R I P S A L P N
C L O O N T E P U U I E
T F R E W R O E N T M
I E S N B E C O H C Y A
O S N N T M R E L H T N
N T U S I L K T O U C H
```

Unused letters:

HOOK MORE FISH WITH THE LURE ENCHANTMENT

MULTIPLAYER MISMATCH

TWIN MOBS

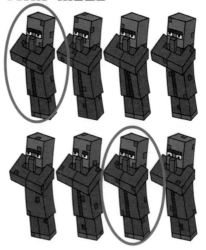

ROTTEN LUCK

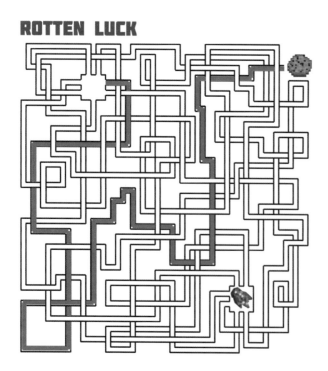

PATH OF DOOM

Gianna - Lava; Mason - Skeleton; Aya - Spider; **Demarco - Creeper**; *Logan - Falling*

TRUTH OR TALE?

Crossword (filled):

```
          F
    Z O M B I E
          S
      W I T H E R
  W I T C H O     
        O C E L O T
        R   F
    G H A S T
        E
```

THE HIGHER THE WOLF'S TAIL,
THE HEALTHIER IT IS

This tall tale (about a tall tail!)
is true.

CONNECT THE DOTS: OUR HERO

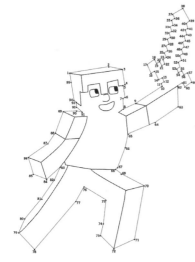

TERMS OF THE GAME

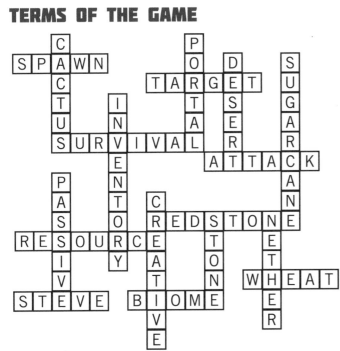

SQUARED UP: INVENTORY

W	S	P	C	M	A
M	C	A	W	S	P
P	A	S	M	C	W
C	M	W	A	P	S
S	W	C	P	A	M
A	P	M	S	W	C

FACT-FINDING MISSION
NAMING A MOB "DINNERBONE"
WILL FLIP IT UPSIDE DOWN
You start in the top left corner.

BLACKOUT

1. N E R V E
2. P I C N I C
3. G R A S S
4. S H A R I N G
5. T H R O W
6. E N D

NIGHT VISION

MULTIPLAYER CTM CHALLENGE
Jillian - Lime; Abi - Magenta;
*Owen - Blue; **Parker - Yellow***

HERE, THERE, AND EVERYWHERE

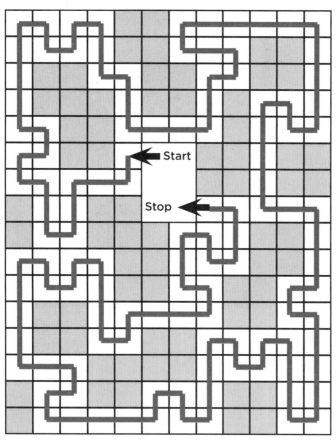

Start

Stop

DOWN ON THE (MOB) FARM

F A R M
H A R M
H A R E
M A R E
M A R S
M A S S
M O S S
M O B S

PLACES, PEOPLE!

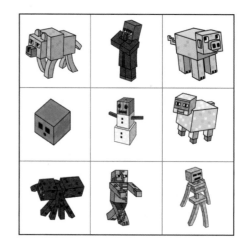

DEFLECT THIS

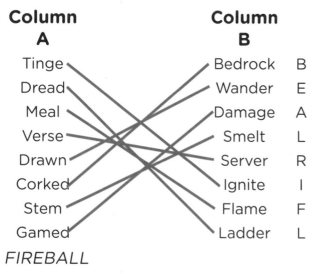

Column A	Column B	
Tinge	Bedrock	B
Dread	Wander	E
Meal	Damage	A
Verse	Smelt	L
Drawn	Server	R
Corked	Ignite	I
Stem	Flame	F
Gamed	Ladder	L

FIREBALL